THE YUMS

Poor Sprout was unhappy

Just look at him frown!

Someone had put him
in the shop

upside-down

He wanted to appear delicious to eat

but all that could be seen were the soles of his feet

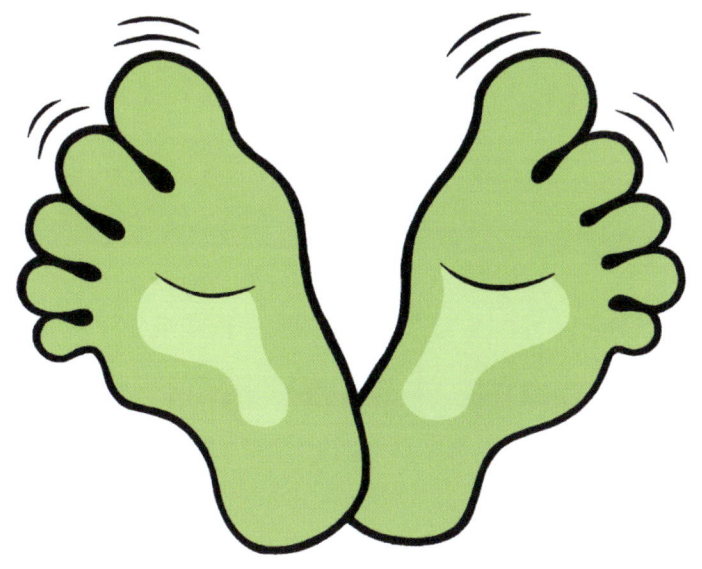

Shoppers walked past with complete disregard

Then suddenly an old lady squeezed him quite hard

'Ooooh! Nice and firm'
She said with such glee

that her false teeth flew out
and bit poor broccoli

The lady bought Sprout and took him home in her trolley

In the bag with his mates he should have felt jolly...

but Sprout feared
that his fate
was to be boiled all day

until he was water-logged
soggy and grey

He might be peeled
by the lady
until tiny and bare

Then he would lose
his vitamins
and need underwear

Or if she left him
under the sink

after a week
he would really stink

But she peeled him with care to his great delight

and cooked Sprout for only 4 minutes

Just right!

Sprout felt like a king
when she crowned him
with butter

and in the bowl
on the table
his heart was a-flutter

Then, oh no!

What horror!

What gloom and doom!

Her grandson Johnny ran into the room

He'll say, 'Yuck'
and pull faces
thought Sprout with despair

He might spit me out
or hide me under a chair

But Sprout's heart
filled with joy
as Johnny did shout

'Yummy Sprouts
make me parp

Everybody watch out!'

Created by Mary Ingram

Read about Sprout's friends...

www.theyums.co.uk

Printed in Great Britain
by Amazon